FLORENCE GRIFFITH JOYNER
OLYMPIC RUNNER

Rob Kirkpatrick

The Rosen Publishing Group's
PowerKids Press™
New York

Published in 2001 by The Rosen Publishing Group, Inc.
29 East 21st Street, New York, NY 10010

First Edition

Book Design: Michael de Guzman

Photo Credits: p. 4 © B. Martin/Allsport; p. 7 © Gerard Vandystadt/Allsport/Vandystadt; pp. 8, 11 Courtesy of California State University–Northridge Sports Information Department; p. 12 Courtesy of UCLA Sports Information Department; p. 15 © Billy Strickland/Allsport; pp. 16, 22 © Tony Duffy/Allsport; p. 19 © Tony Duffy/Allsport and Steve Powell/Allsport; p. 20 © Al Bello/Allsport.

Kirkpatrick, Rob.
      Florence Griffith Joyner : Olympic runner / by Rob Kirkpatrick.
       p. cm. — (Great record breakers in sports)
      Includes index.
      Summary: A biography of the United States Olympic track and field star known as "Flo Jo."
      ISBN 0-8239-5632-6 (lib. bdg.)
      1. Griffith Joyner, Florence Delorez, 1960—Juvenile literature. 2. Runners (Sports)—United States—Biography—Juvenile literature. [1. Griffith Joyner, Florence Delorez, 1960– 2. Runners (Sports) 3. Afro-Americans—Biography. 4. Women—Biography.] I. Title. II. Series.

GV1061.15.G75 K57 2000
796.42'092—dc21
[B]
                                             99-089130

Manufactured in the United States of America

CONTENTS

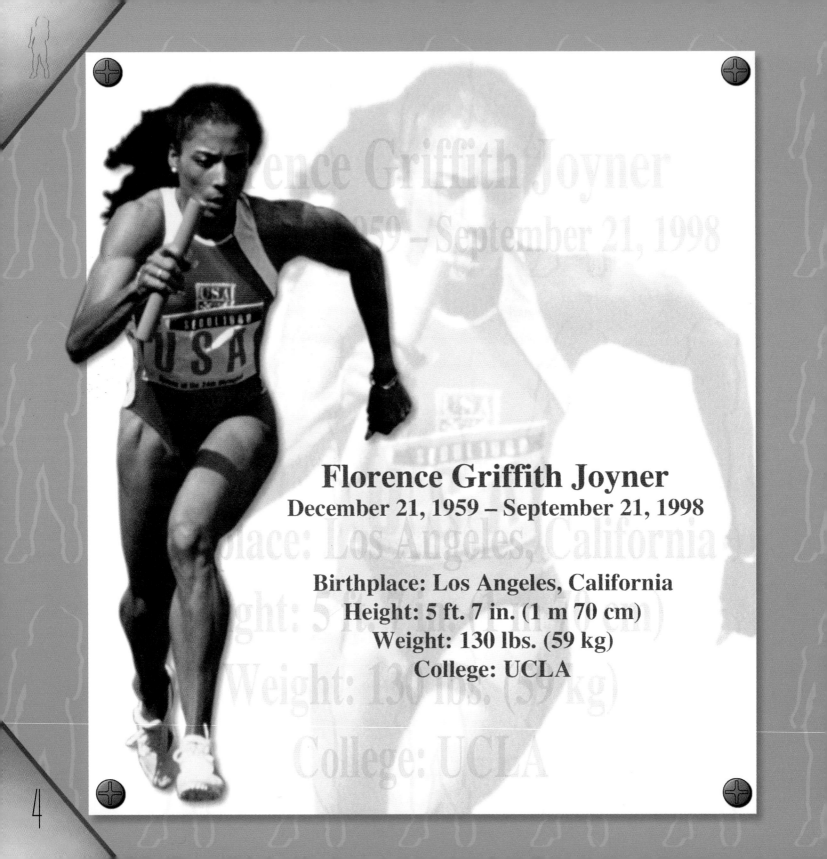

Florence Griffith Joyner
December 21, 1959 – September 21, 1998

Birthplace: Los Angeles, California
Height: 5 ft. 7 in. (1 m 70 cm)
Weight: 130 lbs. (59 kg)
College: UCLA

4

MEET FLORENCE GRIFFITH JOYNER

Have you ever run against other people in a race? Florence Griffith Joyner ran in track races. Track athletes race against each other in races of different distances. Florence ran in 100-, 200-, and 400-meter races. She set **records** in both the 100-meter and 200-meter races. She also ran in **relay races**. In a relay race, four runners make up a team. Each person runs equal legs, or distances, of the race. Only one runner races at a time. The first runner hands off a baton, or stick, to the second runner. The second runner runs the second leg of the race. The second runner then hands off the baton to the third runner, and so on. Florence's team set world records in the 4 x 100-meter relay.

◄ *Florence Griffith Joyner ran in 4 x 100-meter relays. A 4 x 100-meter relay race means that four people ran 100 meters each in the relay race.*

RACING FOR RECORDS

In track races, people keep records to remember who runs the fastest in distance races. It is very exciting for runners when they break records. Runners are very good athletes. The last runner in a race often finishes very close to the runner who finishes first. The finishing times for races can get very close. In 1988, for example, Florence's 4 x 400-meter relay team finished with a time of 3 minutes and 15.51 seconds. This time put them in second place behind the Soviet Union's team, which ran a time of 3 minutes and 15.18 seconds. That is less than half a second difference!

Florence ran the fastest leg of the 4 x 400-meter relay race for the U.S. team in the 1988 Olympics. Still, the ▶ U.S. team lost to the Soviet Union's team that year.

4 x 400 – meter relay
4 x 400 – meter relay
4 x 400 – meter relay
4 x 400 – meter relay
4 x 400 – meter relay

Florence Griffith

A YOUNG RUNNER

Dolorez Florence Griffith was born on December 21, 1959, in Los Angeles, California. Florence, as she was called, started running in races when she was seven years old. It was said that Florence ran like lightning as a child. She went to Jordan High School in Los Angeles. While in high school, she ran on a relay team with three other girls. In 1978, they raced in a 4 x 110-meter relay and won the state championship. Florence's team was faster than any other high school team that year.

◄ *Florence started to run in races when she was seven years old. By the time she was a teenager, she and her high school relay team were winning lots of races.*

PRACTICING FOR THE OLYMPICS

In 1979, Florence attended California State University at Northridge, also called Cal State–Northridge. She was not going there to run track, though. She wanted to learn business. The college's track coach, Bobby Kersee, got Florence to join the team. Florence was such a great runner that she was chosen to go to the 1980 U.S. **Olympic Trials** in Eugene, Oregon. The runners who did the best there got to go to the **Olympic Games** as members of the national team. She finished eighth in the 100-meter race and fourth in the 200-meter race. She did not make the Olympic team, but she came close. She kept training so she could make the team someday.

When Florence started college at Cal State–Northridge, she did not plan to run track. Coach Bobby Kersee helped her change her mind. ▶

Florence Griffith at Cal State-Northridge with her coach, Bob Kersee, and teammates.

A COLLEGE CHAMPION

In 1981, Florence decided to change schools. She went to the University of California, Los Angeles, or UCLA. That year she ran for a relay team in a 4 x 100-meter race in Rome, Italy. Her team finished the race in 42.82 seconds. This broke the American record of 42.87 seconds. In 1982, Florence ran in the **NCAA Championships**. She won the 200-meter race. She also ran on a 4 x 100-meter relay team. This time her team set a new American record by running in 41.47 seconds. In 1983, she won the NCAA Championships in the 400-meter race. She also ran in the 200-meter race and finished second.

◄ *In 1981, Florence became a UCLA student. She also ran in the 4 x 100-meter relay race for the U.S. relay team in Rome, Italy.*

FLORENCE LOVED L.A.

In 1984, Florence made the Olympic team. She came in second in the 200-meter race. She won the **silver medal** at the Olympics. She was now one of the most famous track athletes in the world. After the Olympics, though, she decided she did not want to race anymore. She wanted to be in business, so she worked for a bank full time. In 1987, she decided that she missed racing. She started practicing again. In August 1987, she went to the World Championships in Rome. She finished second in the 200-meter race. She also ran the third leg in the 4 x 100-meter race. Her relay team won the **gold medal** in that race with a time of 41.58 seconds.

Florence and her U.S. teammates won the gold medal in the 4 x 100-meter race.

Flo Jo

1988 Olympic Trials

100 - meter race — **10.49 seconds**
World record

200 - meter race — 21.77 seconds
American record

FLORENCE GETS MARRIED

In October 1987, Florence married Al Joyner in Las Vegas, Nevada. Al had won the gold medal in the 1984 Olympic triple jump. Florence changed her name to Florence Griffith Joyner. Newspaper writers began to shorten her name and call her "Flo Jo." In July 1988, Flo Jo was a star at the Olympic Trials in Indianapolis, Indiana. In the 100-meter race, she broke the world record with a time of 10.49 seconds. Her time was faster than American Evelyn Ashford's 1984 record of 10.76 seconds. Then Flo Jo set a new American record in the 200-meter race with a time of 21.77 seconds. She became one of the most popular athletes in the United States.

◄ *Her coach said that when Florence set her mind to do something, she got the job done. In 1988, she broke the world record in the 100-meter race.*

FLO JO IN SEOUL

Flo Jo became even more well known at the 1988 Olympics in Seoul, South Korea. She broke her own Olympic record in the 100-meter race with a time of 10.54 seconds and won the gold medal. She set a world record in the 200-meter race with a time of 21.34 seconds and won the gold medal. She won a third gold medal with the 4 x 100-meter relay team, which finished in 41.98 seconds. She almost won another gold medal with the 4 x 400-meter relay. Her team finished in second place. The Soviet Union's team finished in first place. Flo Jo got a silver medal for this race. She received a total of four medals at the 1988 Olympics!

At the 1988 Olympics, Flo Jo got three gold medals and a silver medal. ▶

LIFE AFTER RACING

Flo Jo did not run in Olympic or **professional** races after 1988. People did not forget her, though. In 1989, she received the **Amateur** Athletic Union's James E. Sullivan Award for being the best amateur athlete in the United States. After her track career, Flo Jo designed clothing. She even designed uniforms for the Indiana Pacers basketball team. In 1990, she and her husband had a daughter, Mary Ruth Griffith Joyner. In 1993, President Bill Clinton named Florence head of the President's Council on Physical Fitness. She was the first woman to be named to that post. In 1994, because of her interest in helping children, she set up the Florence Griffith Joyner Youth Foundation.

◀ *Florence replaced Arnold Schwarzenegger as head of the President's Council on Physical Fitness in 1993.*

WE WILL REMEMBER FLO JO

In 1998, Flo Jo was busy designing clothing and shoes for a company called Saucony. On September 20, she went to watch a gymnastics meet and then visited her mother. When she got home, she felt tired and went to bed. The next morning, her husband saw that she was not breathing. He called the police. Flo Jo had died of heart failure. She was 38 years old. Her family and friends were very sad. Her fans were sad, too. They will always remember what a great athlete she was. Her speed, talent, and style impressed many people. When you break as many records as Florence Griffith Joyner did, you will never be forgotten.

GLOSSARY

amateur (AM-uh-chur) In sports, an athlete who does not earn money to take part in or play a certain sport.

gold medal (GOHLD MEHD-uhl) The award given for first place.

NCAA Championships (N C A A CHAM-pee-un-ships) The National Collegiate Athletic Association's contests in which college sports teams compete to decide which is the best team in the United States.

Olympic Games (oh-LIHM-pik GAYMS) When the best athletes in the world meet every four years to compete against each other.

Olympic Trials (oh-LIHM-pik TRY-uhls) Contests held to see who is good enough to go to the Olympic Games.

professional (pro-FEH-shuh-nul) In sports, an athlete who earns money to take part in or play a certain sport.

records (REK-urdz) When a player does something better than any other player ever has.

relay races (REE-lay RAYS-ez) Races in which four runners make up a team. Each person runs equal distances. When one runner is done with her part of the race, she passes a baton, or stick, to the next runner who continues to run. That person hands off the baton to the third runner, and so on.

silver medal (SIHL-ver MEHD-uhl) The award given for second place in an Olympic race or contest.

INDEX

WITHDRAWN

WEB SITES

To learn more about Florence Griffith Joyner, check out these Web sites:

http://www.olympic-usa.org/olympians/meet/bios/joyner.html
http://www.usatf.org/athletes/hof/flojo.shtml